Edited by Johnny Rogan
Cover & Book designed by Kalina Owczarek,
4i Limited
Picture research by Nikki Russell

ISBN 0.7119.5157.8
Order No.OP47786

Exclusive Distributors
Book Sales Limited,
8/9 Frith Street,
London W1V 5TZ, UK.

Music Sales Corporation,
257 Park Avenue South,
New York, NY 10010, USA.

Music Sales Pty Limited,
120 Rothschild Avenue, Rosebery,
NSW 2018, Australia.

To the Music Trade only:
Music Sales Limited,
8/9 Frith Street,
London W1V 5TZ, UK.

Eve...
cop...
boo...
We...
concerned would contact us.

Printed in the United Kingdom by
Ebenezer Baylis & Son, Worcester.

A catalogue record for this book is available
from the British Library.

Photo Credits:
Matt Anker/Retna: 8/9, 15, 23; Matt Bright/SIN: 2, 38/39;
Adrian Callaghan/Retna: 14; Joe Dilworth/SIN: 20/21, 32; Steve Double/Retna: 6,
22, 42/43; Steve Double/SIN: 1, 16/17, 40, 48; Patrick Ford/Redferns: 37;
Jill Furmanovsky/Retna: 25; Liane Hentscher/SIN: 5t&b, 29; Alistair Indge/Retna:
10/11, 28; London Features International: front cover, 4, 18, 24, 26/27, 33, 34,
35, 46; Hayley Madden/SIN: 13; Valerie Phillips/Retna: 12; Brian Rasic/Rex
Features: 31, 44, 45t&b; Ed Sirrs/Retna: 19; Dylan Vaughan/SIN: 36.

THE CR

ANBERRIES

It was not often that the head teacher at Ballybricken Primary School stopped classes, so when he tapped the blackboard and called for quiet the whole room lifted their heads to see what was happening. The teacher led a shy, petite girl to the front of class where she clambered on to a graffiti-covered desk top, brushed herself down and started to sing. From that tiny mouth came a voice of angelic and haunting power, heavy with Irish brogue and rich with emotions way beyond her years. Those of such a persuasion said this extraordinary gift was God given.

For five-year-old Dolores Mary Eileen O'Riordan such lofty statements were irrelevant. She just loved to sing, and she did so whenever she could – at church, at school and at home, where she was the youngest of seven children, with one other sister and five brothers. She lived in the tiny village of Ballybricken, eight miles outside Limerick, which was the third largest city of the glorious Irish Republic, rife with unemployment but bolstered by its provincial character. Hers was a traditional and strictly religious Catholic household, and as such the family home was a modest affair, a simple two bedroom farm cottage filled with the smells of cooking, of the chickens and goats outside, and of the sounds of children running around. Soaring above this cacophony was little Dolores' incredible voice, constantly singing. Dolores' father had been forced out of work through a serious injury some years before, so her caterer mother was the only bread winner, making it a Spartan childhood, but nevertheless a happy one.

Dolores' first major trauma came at the age of seven, when her elder sister accidentally burnt down the family home. Fortunately, such was the close-knit and communal nature of the rural village that the local people pooled their spare money and found the O'Riordan family a new and bigger house within weeks. Once in the new house, Dolores began to develop her own strong sense of individuality, strengthened by her family environment. Her mother had a soft spot for the boys, and although she loved the two girls intensely, as the young Dolores grew up she sometimes resented the apparent freedom that was given to her male siblings. They would be allowed to go out late and do all the things that she wanted to do, a restraint which only served to bottle up her increasingly wild nature and turn her into a little tearaway. She wasn't into dolls, pretty dresses or the colourful ribbons that were tied into her hair – she was a tomboy, roughened by the predominantly male environment around her, and especially encouraged by her eldest brother whose exotic lifestyle of cars and girls made him something of a tearaway as well – Dolores adored him. Despite her rebellious streak, she went to church and enjoyed it, singing majestically and amazing the assembled

3

elders – she won many church awards at this early age. However, as she grew up and her defiant nature developed, the admiration turned to consternation, especially when she turned up one day in brightly coloured odd socks, an act intended to win some respect for her strong individuality, but one which simply earned her a mighty scolding once back at home.

At school Dolores was never top of the class, but she enjoyed learning about Ireland's rich history, and was comfortable with all the lessons being taught in the native Gaelic tongue. Her academic grades were quite good, but she preferred the Irish music and jig dancing to study, and even learnt to play the tin whistle. In her early teens she was given classical piano lessons and this fuelled her growing musical passion, and more importantly gave her the knowledge to start creating her own compositions – very soon she became known at school as 'the girl who wrote songs'. She still hung out mostly with boys, usually her brothers, principally because there were not that many girls to befriend in such a small village. It wasn't long before she wrote her first song, 'Calling', about a crush she had developed on a local middle aged man.

"The so...
potentia...
because...
were, th...
they we...

6

A few miles away in the equally small town of Moycross, the family bakers had two similarly musical children – the young Hogan brothers were always busy learning guitar and listening to music. When the American teen movie *Breakin'* arrived, detailing the colourful world of break dancing, tracksuits and boomboxes, the brothers Mike and Noel were entranced. Every Saturday they would run down to the main park in Limerick to join the hundreds of kids who gathered there to show off their new found dancing skills. It was here that the two youngsters met a boy from

sing a bit. Apparently. It was 1990.

Leaving them with only a name and possibly one of the greatest ever musical understatements, Niall left the band. The following week, the Hogans were approached by one Dolores O'Riordan, now 18, who had already heard of the vacancy and was eager to join the group in order to soften the tedium of her part-time shop job. She had been looking for a decent band for four years now, and had even played in a few sub-standard cover outfits, but their lack of ambition and the monotony of the £50-a-night pub circuit

s were not to my taste, but I saw the
the playing. It was easy for me
matter what their first impressions
minute I opened my mouth I knew that
going to be impressed."

nearby Parteen, called Feargal Lawler, and despite him being a year older, their common love for music soon cemented a close friendship. Feargal was stumbling his way through the rigours of learning the drums, so the logical thing seemed to be to form a band, and this they did when the Hogans were aged 18, inspired principally by The Smiths and bedecked in bedraggled haircuts and scruffy clothes. With Mike adopting the bass and Noel mastering the guitar, all they needed was a singer.

'My Granny Drowned In A Fountain At Lourdes' may not be the most conventional nor serious of titles for a song, but it was enough to enlist the vocal talents of their friend Niall, whose outlandish character and oddball sense of humour perfectly fitted their need for a confident lead man – the completed line-up promptly called themselves Cranberry Saw Us, a dreadful pun on the traditional Christmas condiment. Unfortunately, once in the band, Niall's comical output worsened, and after penning such minor classics as 'Throw Me Down A Big Stairs' and 'Good Morning God', he realised that his novel ditties were not really appreciated and so decided to leave. Since the departure was on amicable terms, he offered to help the Hogans and Feargal locate a new singer. He came up with a typically tenuous suggestion – his girlfriend's sister had a mate who could

frustrated her loftier ambitions. Having now left home, Dolores' confidence was growing. Mike and Noel arranged an audition and when the day arrived she walked in with a keyboard under her tiny arm, a crop of dark hair, and an overwhelming confidence in her ability to sing – she was not one to be intimidated by the room full of boys (she had been in this situation all her life). Cranberry Saw Us played her some material, and although she wasn't bowled over, she still wanted in. Dolores later said of that first meeting: "The songs were not to my taste, but I saw the potential in the playing. It was easy for me because no matter what their first impressions were, the minute I opened my mouth I knew that they were going to be impressed."

Needless to say, in the words of Niall, she could indeed 'sing a bit' and seemed very committed, with not a shred of 'girlyness' in her (the band had feared this). Thus, Dolores was duly taken on board, as was her suggestion that they shorten the name to The Cranberries. She took home a demo tape of some rough material, mostly just chord sequences and, inspired by the freedom in the music, she began to write some lyrics and overlay melodies. Within the week, she went back to the band with a handful of completed songs, which were then recorded on to tape. Although the demos they made were very crude, there was enough to indicate that they had hit on a good combination – her personal lyrics and phenomenal voice mixed well with the bare bones accompaniment of the three Smiths aficionados. The first song they played as a new band was the beautiful 'Linger' which, within four years, would become an international smash hit across the world.

The Cranberries started rehearsing three times a week. At this stage the band had taken the unusual step of deliberately aiming towards recording their songs, rather than playing them live as most bands prefer. However, they also knew they would need to play live at some stage, so they nervously booked their début gig at a club called Ruby's, situated in the basement of a hotel. Here they played in front of 60 people, performing only six terror-stricken songs – the ordeal for these chronically shy teenagers was so bad that they turned their heads away from the crowd at all times, looking as if they would crumble if anyone managed to make eye contact. A handful of gigs followed at various small local venues in Limerick, Dublin and Cork, after which their minds turned to rehearsing for the demo which they had been so focused upon. The quiet guitarist Noel found it difficult to talk to people, so quite often they would just play and play, with very few words shared between them. As a result of this arrangement a close musical relationship started to develop between Dolores and Noel which quickly became highly productive. Within weeks of first meeting Dolores they had enough songs for a proper demo.

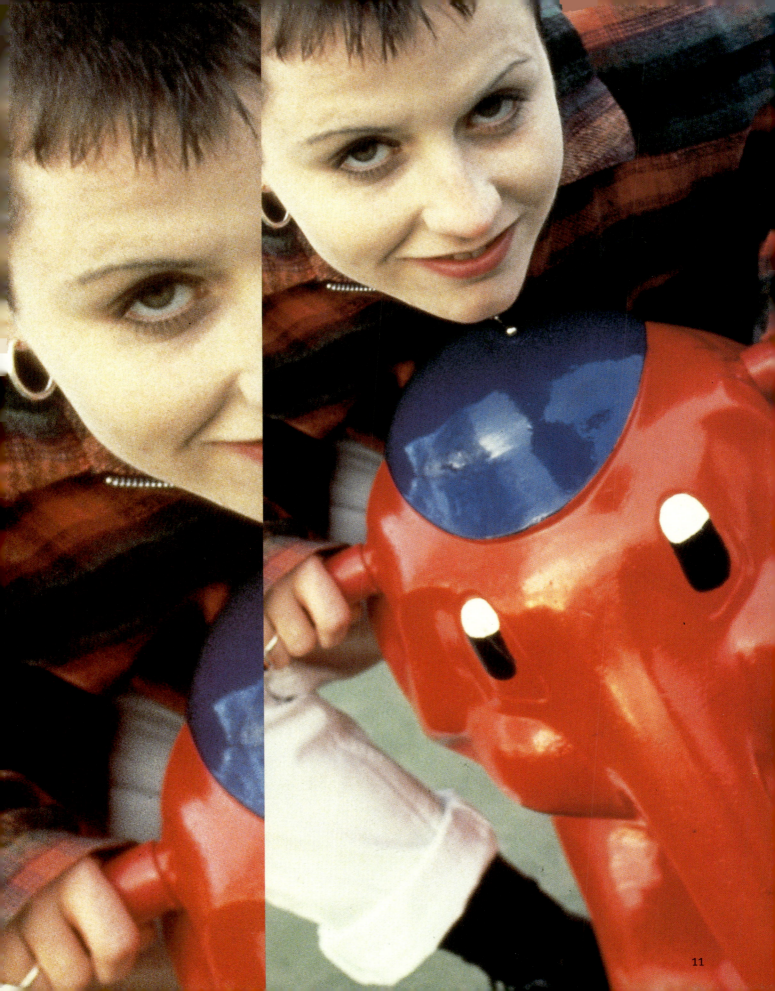

At one of their first gigs they had met a local entrepreneur and frontman for the band Private World, Pearse Gilmore, who had offered to help them record the demo, and soon after became their manager. It was a premature decision which the fledgling band would come to bitterly regret. For now however, Gilmore offered them a guiding hand and the modest studio facilities of his own small independent record label Xeric, which was based in a disused factory in suburban Limerick. Here, they recorded a three-track demo which they called 'Nothing Left At All' (the title track would re-surface a year later on the B-side of their first single). Posters were plastered all over town for the tape announcing that it was "a first glimpse of a bigger picture", and, despite their timid live shows to date, they still managed to sell over 300 copies in local shops. It was a good response, but nothing compared to the astonishing reaction their demo tape would create in the music industry.

The hand written inlay (the band name was spelt Cranberry's at this stage) listed five tracks which included 'Linger' and 'Dreams'. Noel Hogan had given up his job fixing cash registers and made the most of his new found dole money and free time to mail out tapes to record companies and radio stations. Thousands of bands do this every week, then wait months before a fraction of the record companies bother to send them a standard rejection letter. However, The Cranberries received highly positive responses within the week from Rough Trade, EMI, Virgin, and Imago (a nascent offshoot of Island). Rough Trade asked them to come to England and play a London show, but the band simply could not afford this.

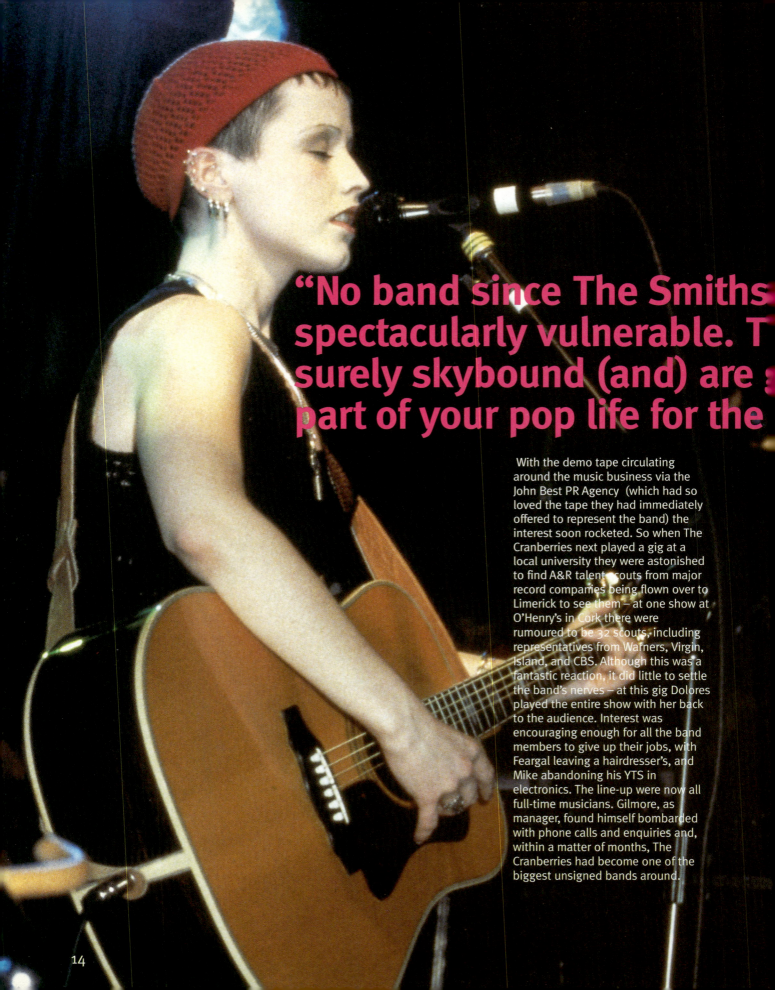

"No band since The Smiths spectacularly vulnerable. T surely skybound (and) are part of your pop life for the

With the demo tape circulating around the music business via the John Best PR Agency (which had so loved the tape they had immediately offered to represent the band) the interest soon rocketed. So when The Cranberries next played a gig at a local university they were astonished to find A&R talent scouts from major record companies being flown over to Limerick to see them – at one show at O'Henry's in Cork there were rumoured to be 32 scouts, including representatives from Warners, Virgin, Island, and CBS. Although this was a fantastic reaction, it did little to settle the band's nerves – at this gig Dolores played the entire show with her back to the audience. Interest was encouraging enough for all the band members to give up their jobs, with Feargal leaving a hairdresser's, and Mike abandoning his YTS in electronics. The line-up were now all full-time musicians. Gilmore, as manager, found himself bombarded with phone calls and enquiries and, within a matter of months, The Cranberries had become one of the biggest unsigned bands around.

ave sounded so
Cranberries are
ing to be a big
ext eternity."

The demo tape itself shimmered with the frailest charm, caressed by Dolores' heavenly vocals, and filled with melancholic observations of a remarkably open nature. 'Nothing Left At All' delved deep into Dolores' private life with beguiling frankness, while 'Put Me Down' was compelling and haunting. The tempo was raised for the delightful celebration of 'Dreams', but the tape's highlight was the phenomenal 'Linger', an intoxicating wondrous waltz detailing a dying relationship and the man's cruel refusal to end the sham. Throughout the five songs, Dolores' voice displayed a truly astonishing range and gentle power – for a band's first sampler, it was simply awesome.

Inevitably the British music press caught wind of a new find, and when they heard the demo tape they knew that here indeed was a genuine new talent. They showered the band with high praise, and despite their lack of a deal they were unofficially cited as the best new band in Britain. One piece in the *Melody Maker* said they had produced "the most exciting demo tape of 1991" adding, "No band since The Smiths have sounded so spectacularly vulnerable. The Cranberries are surely skybound (and) are going to be a big part of your pop life for the next eternity." With grunge on its way over from Seattle and the British music scene deep into bands like Ride, Swervedriver, The Boo Radleys and Chapterhouse, The Cranberries were a breath of fresh air. Their relatively sheltered background accentuated their unique sound – at a time when the so-called 'shoe-gazing' scene was the height of informed fashion, The Cranberries were absolutely ignorant of anything remotely cool, or musically fashionable – they were four anonymous teenagers whose crude demo tape of raw talent had wowed the London music business. Word of mouth about this great new find spread quickly. They were suddenly press darlings, and during the spring and summer of 1991 were fêted in all the music media, which talked of them in reverential terms, which was ironic since at this stage all they actually had

were six songs and a poor live show. As Dolores recalls, they were "four timid little teenagers, front person standing sideways like a statue, afraid to budge in case she tripped and fell. We weren't performers at that stage, but it was the potential they saw."

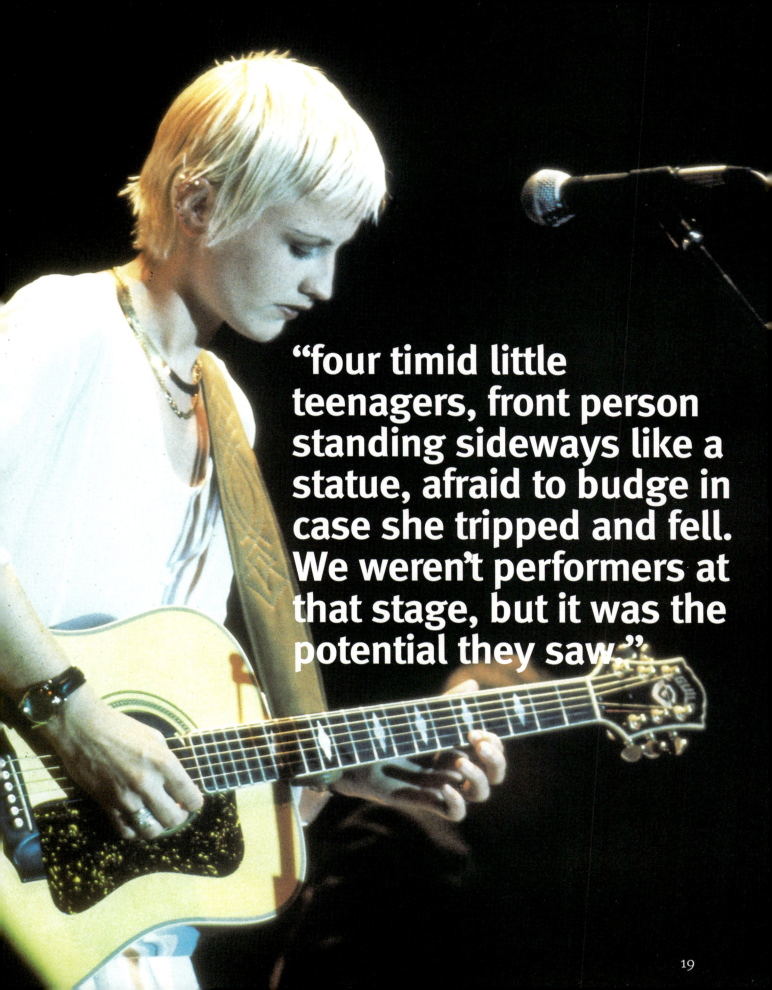

"four timid little teenagers, front person standing sideways like a statue, afraid to budge in case she tripped and fell. We weren't performers at that stage, but it was the potential they saw."

Of all the record companies keen to tap into that potential, Island won the race to sign The Cranberries to a six-album deal, although only after some internal disagreements within the band, which were eventually resolved by democratic vote and the sheer weight of Island's reputation. So the infant group now found themselves with a recording contract and a hyped reputation that meant they could seemingly do no wrong. All seemed to be going incredibly well, and it would have been reasonable for them to have expected the next year or so to be one long series of successes. They could not have been more wrong. Within 12 months they would become embroiled in a vicious legal battle while their début single would be ridiculed by the press, which would soon shun them completely.

A series of events then occurred that took The Cranberries from prodigious new talent and flavour of the month to musical outcasts, eschewed by the very same people who only weeks earlier had praised them unconditionally. Firstly, their début EP release proved to be an enormous disappointment, especially when compared to the remarkable demo that had been responsible for so much interest in the first place. 'Uncertain' was rush released on Xeric Records, through Island, in October 1991, but rather than receive the high praise they were already used to, it was derided as weak and derivative, which indeed it was. Gilmore's forceful hand had dominated the recording and The Cranberries' unique sound had been relegated to what amounted to a fashion statement, cluttered with contemporaneous, shuffling dance beats and vogue guitar, with a muddy mix drowning out the all-important Dolores vocals. It was a very poor, second grade release and the press were very unforgiving.

The stifling degree of control which Gilmore seemed determined to exert on the band's career was the second setback which the group experienced at this time. He simply had too much influence – he managed them, produced their records, took their promo photographs, controlled the stock of their records, and allegedly sank much of the Island record deal advance into upgrading his own studio. He even turned down potential help. When Rough Trade had enquired about the band when they were still unsigned, Gilmore feared for his position and refused to return any calls or arrange any meetings. In his ill-placed desire to control every aspect of the band he was in fact throttling them – while their label-mates PJ Harvey and Stereo MC's spectacularly stormed ahead, The Cranberries were hurtling backwards.

The third nail in the coffin at this point was the band's poor live show, which was exacerbated by poor management strategy. Two three-week UK tours in the summer of 1991, with the Scouse stompers Top and the morose Moose, were ill-advised choices, and the band's apparent terror at playing live disappointed the expectant hordes who gathered to see this latest best thing. Tour budgets and plans made matters worse – Dolores was frequently forced to sleep across the laps of the band in the bus, hardly ideal conditions from which to produce her astonishing vocal performances. Mediocre gear and squalid touring conditions heightened the problems and shows suffered as a result. When the band arrived in London to play their first gig after signing to Island, at The Camden Underworld, the media were not impressed. The show was crammed with industry insiders, and you could count the number of 'normal' punters on one hand, a sign that the band were indeed very big news in a very small world.

Unfortunately this was not their night and it cost them dearly. The *Melody Maker* again led the attack: "What has been trumpeted as the latest and greatest is in reality a mess, the crowd play a game of spot-the-reference and we're ransacking the Thesaurus for new ways to say 'Disappointed'."

While it is one thing for the media to criticise an incompetent performance, it is quite another to adopt a patronising tone with regard to The Cranberries' inexperience and nationality, and in this regard the UK music press acted shamefully. Had an English band appeared at such an early age, writing such heart-breaking and intense music, matters would no doubt have been different. As it stood, The Cranberries' emotive music was put to one side as they were portrayed as four simple yokels, naïve leprechauns with a charming innocence and small town view. One paper headlined the feature on the band "Yo! Bumpkin Rush the Show", while another abused the trust Dolores had shown when letting them see her home by describing her abode as if it was straight out of the film *My Left Foot,* slyly forgetting to mention the microwave, TV, video and various other modern fittings. Another talked only half-jokingly of "four little leprechauns from Ireland wearing green hats with bows on the top, who don't have a clue" and of "naïve starry-eyed children". Still another story recounted mockingly how one night on their first band trip in a London hotel, they had drunk the mini-bars and subsequent refills dry because they thought it was all free, and had then been shocked to receive a bill for the alcohol of £460 each.

To be fair to the press, the band did themselves few favours, with Dolores confessing that until she had been to London with her Dad aged 15, she had never seen a black man and also that she was a chain crisp eater. Hardly the sort of coverage that makes the public take a band too seriously. As a result, every piece on The Cranberries was plastered in words like 'naïve', 'innocent', 'honest' and 'pure', and this portrayal was used to simplify their music and lyrics. The damage was severe. It was as if the press felt the band was unaware they were making this wonderful music, such was their naïveté.

From a media guilty of classing Irish bands as either mystical Gods or drunken hicks, The Cranberries were labelled both. This annoyed them immensely, and Dolores later said of the whole approach that "Just because every second word isn't fuck and every song isn't about sexual intercourse, people think it's innocent." Eventually, the band had to' force themselves to stop reading the music papers. This did not stop the rot. By the time the disappointing début 'Uncertain' EP came out, there was already a backlash, and within a matter of weeks, The Cranberries were old and best forgotten news.

To make matters worse, when the band came to record their début album in January 1992 at Xeric Studios, the situation with their manager Gilmore had become intolerable. Once again his Svengali ambitions meant that he cluttered the mixes, this time with dance beats and industrial guitars, and his continued dictatorial studio approach increased the tension between him and the band until it finally became unworkable – in four weeks of tense recordings they managed only three sub-standard songs. They were barely on speaking terms and the atmosphere deteriorated so badly that they had to make the break – they sacked him. By now, the series of seemingly endless disasters had taken its toll on the band, and especially on Dolores. She was slipping into abject depression and the whole fiasco had driven her to bed, made her very ill and induced dramatic weight loss. She had found out to her cost that the claustrophobic nature of the London music scene was equally as stifling as the provincial insularity of her home town. It was the low point of their career and one that she is not likely to forget, as she explained to *Melody Maker*: "It really made me very ill, very young. It was a terrible thing to happen, but I learnt so much about life that way. I learned by getting sick, and what I did to myself in that state of mind, that I had the power in my mind not to let myself get that bad again... It was my baby version of what happened to Kurt Cobain, to Sinéad O'Connor." Things looked serious and she contemplated leaving the band – at this stage it seemed like the only sensible thing to do: "I couldn't take it any more. I couldn't even get out of bed any more. I discovered that life's not a sweet trip at all. It seemed to me to be the biggest farce. All I ever wanted to do was write songs and be a singer without being hurt by the industry. I just freaked." She was still only 19.

Most of 1992 was spent picking up the pieces from the disastrous string of events that had so devastated the band the previous year. After a brief period of self-management, The Cranberries teamed up with Geoff Travis, head of Rough Trade Records, the label that had taken such an interest in the group before anyone else (although it had actually been Travis' colleague Sarah Bolton who had heard the demo tape). Travis had been following the band since their inception and had cringed at their managerial problems and media mismanagement – he knew there was far more to The Cranberries than the crippling 'new Sundays/Sinéad/Bjork' tag with which many had labelled them.

Indeed, at this stage, Travis took Dolores to one side and told her: "People react to your songs exactly the way they did to Morrissey's songs." The first thing he did was to extricate Gilmore from any future involvement with The Cranberries – it was not until 1995 that the legal repercussions of this debacle had fully worked themselves out and the band were finally and completely free (one condition is that neither The Cranberries nor Gilmore are allowed to talk to the press about their disagreements). The second thing Travis did was to scrap what passed for the début album thus far, and re-start the whole project from scratch. He sent the band to Windmill Studios in Dublin and appointed Stephen Street as producer, a man with the eminent qualifications of having engineered and produced The Smiths' last three albums. Noel Hogan had initially called Johnny Marr and asked if he would produce the record but received a polite refusal.

Once at the studio, Street was struck by how the band's recent difficulties had reflected on their musicality as a group, and was concerned that they were far too incoherent to record an album, lacking the necessary musical unity. So he set about encouraging them to play together again, to heal the wounds caused by the previous year's troubles. As the project progressed, it became clear that his sympathetic and gently subtle production approach suited the band perfectly, and the sessions went very well. By the time the album was finished, The Cranberries had produced a record that would eventually become a runaway international hit, selling over 3.5 million copies world-wide.

The album was a highly personal diary of desire being ripped open, and of passion thwarted – a documentation of some of the betrayals that had sometimes made Dolores physically ill.

The record's anguished sensuality told the story of one woman's painful failures as a young girl and her later rebirth as an adult, and carried with it all the ensuing hurt, emotional trauma, shattered hope and upset involved in the cruel games that lovers play, emphasised by the sense that this was a repressed creative force finally opening her heart to the cruel world. Although the album was credited as co-written, the lyrical focus was very much O'Riordan's. Her independence showed through on 'Put Me Down' which was a simmering diatribe against a clearly sexist victim, while on 'Pretty' she vented her anger against those people in the business who made her feel less than she was. There was a happier side too, with the exuberant 'Dreams' and the intoxicating 'Sunday', tracks which were delightful attempts at catching that very moment when someone feels exquisite joy. And of course, in 'Linger' the band had their trump card, with perhaps one of the most incisive, mournful songs about the death throes of love ever written. Dolores showed an ability to bring fleeting passions and emotions strongly into focus, clearing confusion with a sudden truth. The openness throughout was almost disarming, making the listener feel uncomfortable, like a voyeur secretly watching her crushing struggles unnoticed; this frankness perhaps reflected Dolores' background, in that she was maybe a little too open, too honest. She later admitted that it was indeed a very personal record: "I know exactly what every song on that album was about. And I know exactly what night I wrote it on and why I wrote it. They elaborate very much how I felt at that time." As for being too honest and open, she also later conceded there was perhaps some ground in this: "I never did anything stupid like take my clothes off. I was always pretty together, but my knowledge of the world was nil – so sometimes I maybe just opened my heart to people I shouldn't have."

Maybe, but it still made for fascinating listening.

The lyrical focus was delivered with a series of immaculately conceived melodies, crystalline production, tasteful music and of course *that* voice, all factors which were arranged with effortless grace. The deluge of melancholic love songs and the wonderful economy of the guitar work (reflecting Hogan's Marr/Smiths influences) made it a simple yet very powerful record that resonated very deep. There was some degree of Gaelic flavour, especially with Dolores' falsetto waterfalls, but enough uniqueness remained to avoid this label and for that matter any other – this, in many senses, was a deeply unfashionable record. Even so, it was a superb début.

With the clumsy title *Everybody Else Is Doing It, So Why Can't We* scrawled across the bottom of an apologetic and dark band shot, The Cranberries' début album should have seen them rightly returned to the pedestal of one of Britain's leading lights. Unfortunately, it seemed their troubles were not yet over. On the album's release in March 1993 (originally scheduled for October, 1992, but there had been more delay until Gilmore's claws were finally removed from the band) the reaction was one of general indifference and only very reserved and conservative approval. Despite 'Dreams' being awarded Single of the Week in *Melody Maker* in November 1992, it did not sell well, while its follow up 'Linger' in February amazingly only reached No. 74, both of which were poor precedents for the forthcoming album. The simple fact was that despite the quality of the release, the record company and the media had moved on; they had found new bands and forgotten The Cranberries. For a group that had promised so much way back in early 1991, the wait for the début album had been too long and, no matter how good the record was, the momentum had been completely lost. The album only reached No. 78 in the charts and sold a meagre 12,000 – it was a flop. What was more, The Cranberries were now faced with almost an entire year on the road, touring an album that had apparently already failed. If the UK had rejected them so flatly, what chance would The Cranberries have in the world's biggest market of all, America?

"I never did anything stupid like take my clothes off. I was always pretty together but my knowledge of the world was nil so sometimes I maybe just opened my heart to people I shouldn't have"

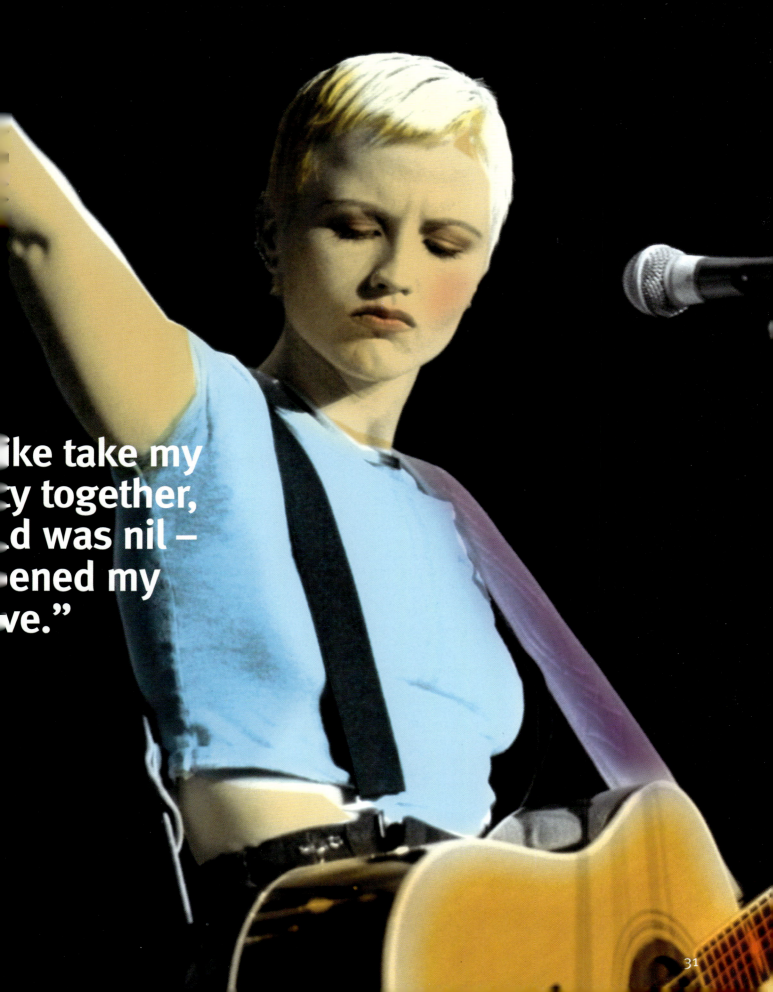

ike take my
y together,
d was nil –
ened my
ve."

The year's hard work started with a credible tour, supporting the highly acclaimed Belly, led by ex-Throwing Muses Tanya Donnely, with whom Dolores sang an encore at the London show at ULU. This was part of Travis' desire to see them become more choosy about their touring partners, so that they would be taken more seriously. The approach certainly seemed to work, as they were soon asked to support Hothouse Flowers in Europe, after which they played a series of dates supporting Mike Oldfield at the Royal Albert Hall. Then, in June, they flew out to America for the start of a six-week tour with The The, starting in Colorado and taking them right across the country. A week before these dates began, their doomed début album had finally been released in America, and with that release a very odd thing started to happen. As the band worked their way across America in support of Matt Johnson's project, album sales started to rise dramatically. At first, *Everybody Else...* was selling a modest 20,000 or so a week, which was still a relative success when compared to their initial UK response. But then, as the dates continued, they sold 30,000 one week, then 50,000 another, and soon things started to go ballistic. By the time they had finished the dates with The The there was already enough interest from the tour and the now extensive radio play they were commanding to justify a few dates of their own. Still more success awaited the release of the two singles, with 'Dreams' leading the way by smashing into the *Billboard* Top 40. *Come September*, the video for the equally successful 'Linger' was featuring heavily on MTV and album sales had rocketed to 75,000 a week (Michael Stipe of R.E.M. turned up to the video shoot for 'Linger').

Meanwhile, the headliners for The Cranberries' next tour, Suede, arrived in the US, promoted as the next great thing from the UK, a dangerous millstone, as The Cranberries well knew. Brett Anderson immediately and ill-advisedly announced that "the US is a thing to be broken, like a disobedient child". After Suede pulled the first three dates and The Cranberries sold out the 2,000-seater venues on their own, their success just spiralled.

Gradually people began to realise that after The Cranberries had finished their support set, people were leaving the venue in droves, well before the unfortunate Suede even walked on stage. As the tour progressed, it became clear that most of the crowd were there exclusively to see The Cranberries. By now, the album was flying off the shelves and MTV was saturating their videos.

This remarkable run of success came to a head in Atlanta, when the sheer weight of public opinion forced the promoters to reverse the bill order, and install The Cranberries as headliners – 4,000 people had turned up to a 2,000-seater venue and the gig itself had to be played outside. It was a humbling experience for Suede, but for The Cranberries it was a fantastic success. This accomplished band, led by an elfin woman with a voice to stop you in your tracks, was winning over converts in their thousands with each new day. From this, the band then went on tour for yet another six weeks with Duran Duran, where the audience reactions were similarly frenzied. By the end of the year, *Everybody Else...* had sold an unbelievable 1.5

million copies in America. From the ashes of their own disaster, The Cranberries had worked up to a crescendo of success unrivalled by British bands at that time – as yet they had still not secured a single front cover of any British music magazine.

Just how the band had achieved this remarkable success is very clear. Most importantly, they toured long and hard throughout 1993, playing second fiddle to bands, but learning their craft along the way and honing their once feeble live show into a formidable and moving exhibition – poor live shows had cost The Sundays dearly and led to them failing in America. Dolores herself was now infinitely more confident on stage and had come to terms with her role as frontwoman. She was happy chatting to the audience, even coaxing them to sing along. Although the band stood still for most of the set, they were becoming far more relaxed and the music benefited as a result. This touring environment was helped enormously by the insular and close-knit touring crew the band took on the road. The self-contained travelling community consisting of old friends

and close colleagues meant they were happy on the road and therefore better on stage. Also, the lack of promotion and media build-up meant that the public found The Cranberries' music for themselves, without any of the hype and pressure that had forced bands like Suede down their throats. Thirdly, The Cranberries' music fitted seamlessly into the middle American radio programming system, alongside such massive acts as Bon Jovi and Madonna, an achievement which many peculiarly English bands had failed to accomplish – Carter USM's South London based tragi-comedies for example will probably never translate wholesale to America. The Cranberries music was seen to have an AOR appeal, a form which has such a massive potential in the States, and Dolores' lyrics were not drenched in the English humour and irony that cripples so much British music. Another aspect of their attraction was the band's inherent Irishness and Celtic spirituality. With so much of the American public hankering after some Irish ancestry, this worked in the band's favour, as opposed to in the UK where it was perhaps seen as a

negative point. At the same time some US fans thought Limerick was in England, so this Irish connection did not account for all of the success. Another element was that the American market cares little for the fashion nuances of British music, and the relative importance of Suede compared to Ride counted for absolutely nothing. Audiences were far more open-minded and the band benefited enormously from that. As Dolores herself says of America: "I love it over there. It's got so much going for it that Europe hasn't... I love the open-mindedness of Americans."

As ever, there was always the attraction of Dolores herself. With the band content to play a lower profile (without which she would have been nothing), this enabled her to attract more attention, and as her confidence grew, she developed into a genuine star in the making. A sign of this had been shown at the Rock Garden in Dublin nearly a year earlier, when the band had played their first gig in months, still reeling from all the difficulties – that night she had been a revelation, smiling and talking with the crowd, for all the world looking

the part of a natural star, rather than a chronically shy girl. Now, with a year on the road in America behind them, The Cranberries presented a confident and thoroughbred show. In addition, Dolores' intense spirituality both spooked and fascinated the Americans – when she said she had always known she would be successful in America they were entranced: "I've known since I was a kid that I was going to be really successful – that's why I was given this voice – so that everyone would hear it."

The contradictions in her also captivated audiences. There was a paradox between the intensely emotive and cerebral lyrics and her often skimpy dresses and suggestive imagery. Finally, The Cranberries were unheard of in America before 1993, so all the preconceptions and press-darlings-turned-failures stigma attached to them in the UK was nowhere to be seen. Ironically, the fact that they were briefly hip in 1991 now worked in their favour – their distinct lack of fashion sense gave them a flavour and originality that set them apart from everyone else. Their failed stab at coolness was now indeed a blessing in disguise. The Cranberries, the pedigrees who had become the runts of the litter, were once again top dog.

Such was the phenomenal success of the album in America, that Island were prompted to re-release the record back in the UK in March 1994, and this time it was a very different story. With the knock-on effect of sales and reputation that success in the States brings, the début album hit the No.1 spot and very quickly went platinum. The two singles 'Dreams' and 'Linger' which were by now over four years old, both charted highly, pre-empting the album's renewed success. With the album occupying the top spot, The Cranberries became only the fifth

band ever to achieve a re-entry at No.1, alongside T Rex, Elvis Presley, the *Fame* soundtrack, and Mike Oldfield's *Tubular Bells*, fine company indeed. With the album sales exceeding three million world-wide, (and 400,000 in the UK alone) the band also won the Best New Irish Band at IRMA awards, a rather belated recognition of their achievements from a reluctant Irish media, which had been quite derisory in the past. The Cranberries were now the only Irish band to sell over one million copies of their début album in the USA, and *Everyone Else...* was the biggest selling début of any British band in 1993. In the same month, they were also voted Top New International Act at the *Music Week* Awards in London.

The change in confidence that some had witnessed in America was now in full flow. Dolores was a changed woman – she had dyed her hair platinum blonde, donned false eyelashes and nine ear rings in one ear alone, turning herself into something of an opaque-eyed temptress. This could not have been more evident than at the gig they played at London's LA2 in January 1994. As if to reinforce the band's success across the Atlantic and remind the on-lookers about how badly they had been treated at home, she waltzed on to the stage draped in the stars and stripes of the American flag, a symbol of the fact that they now had the world's biggest market at their feet. During this show it became clear why The Cranberries' live performance had captivated so many people and sold so many records. They were no longer innocents pleading for a chance, and she was no longer a shrinking violet, afraid of her own shadow. She was now a whirling stomping front woman, cajoling the crowd while the nonchalant men behind her produced crisp and sweet accompaniment. Dolores' told *Melody Maker* that the transformation from shy teenagers to rock monsters was borne of their hard touring and of her assuming more control through experience: "I knew that so much of performing was false, and I didn't like being in a position where a lot of people were looking at me, Dolores. I felt vulnerable up there. But then it reversed!!"

The Cranberries were now firmly ensconced as one of Britain's most successful bands of the Nineties, solely on the strength of their début album. The time had come for a follow up. After all, some of the original 12 songs had been penned way back in

1991 and there was a danger that people would feel they were milking their material too much. Fortunately, the year touring America and the subsequent colossal success had inspired Dolores with hordes of new material, and by February 1994 the whole second album's worth of material was ready. Just eight months after their début album finally hit the No.1 spot in the British charts, The Cranberries released its successor, entitled *No Need To Argue*. Prior to its release, they had planned to play some dates with Crowded House but a severe leg injury to Dolores as a result of a serious skiing accident put paid to that. She hit a pole at speed and tore her anterior cruciate ligament, an injury sufficiently serious to finish a sportsman's career. Metal pins and plates had to be inserted into her knee and the tour with Crowded House was the inevitable victim of this unforeseen problem. She now feels that this injury was in fact a blessing in disguise, as it forced her to take time off which, in turn, gave her a chance to reflect on what had happened and put things into perspective.

Another event between the belated success of *Everyone Else...* and the follow-up, was Dolores' marriage to Don Burton, the production manager for Duran Duran whom she had met while the band were supporting the Birmingham popsters in America during 1993. Dolores had suffered more than most through bitter relationships, and the year 1992 was particularly damaging, especially when added to all the problems the band had experienced. So when she met Burton, a self-assured and stylishly handsome Canadian seven years her senior, she fell deeply in love. Here at last appeared to be a soul mate for her, and such was her adoration that she took in his three-year-old child as her own. The romance was intense and a whirlwind courtship was soon followed by a wedding in front of 200 guests and hundreds of Irish paparazzi and on-lookers at Holy Cross Abbey monastery in County Tipperary. The happy couple rode in on white horses with cascades of flowers adorning the carriages, and when Dolores stepped out it was to reveal her spectacular bridal wear. It was a full Pope-upsetting regalia, with white skimpy knickers showing through her lace leggings, a small tube top and a gemstone in her exposed belly button. When the sensational wedding shots flashed across the papers, many Irish traditionalists were outraged, and local radio stations received many complaints talking of her 'disrespect for the Church' and her 'vulgarity'. For her own part, Dolores was still a keen Catholic, and did not see that wearing what she wanted to on her wedding day made her any less religious. She recalled how her father had come to see her dress and when she unveiled the white bikini and navel jewel he had said "That's beautiful, but where's the dress?" By getting hitched in her knickers, Dolores became a media icon for the day, which only increased the public attention which was already on her, but since that day she has confirmed that she is in wedlock for life, and that she has never been happier. In late 1994, the newly-weds began building a family home in County Kerry far from the city in a Gaeltacht area, that is, one where the locals still speak Gaelic.

When the second album was released in October 1994, it was a much darker document than its predecessor, and the songs were far more mature and crafted, making this an accomplished record by any standards. It was written largely on the road in 1993 while they toured America, and the white knuckle ride of meteoric fame which has killed so many bands affected the material indelibly. Dolores' lyrics were already road weary and in many senses very negative, disturbingly so for one who was still only 23 years old. Inevitably, this album was stamped with the manifold changes that the band had experienced as a result of their world-wide travel and older years. Noticeably, the album was devoid of hope on most tracks, a desperate and miserable affair for the most part, perhaps a reflection of the big bad world they had encountered once they had travelled beyond the boundaries of Limerick which had inspired the more pure material on the début. Here we find loneliness, tears, fear, betrayal, emptiness, disappointment, doubt, a grossly unhappy record immersed in her many cries for help. The personal nature was emphasised by the scratchy handwriting in which the lyrics were displayed on the sleeve, like extracts from her own private diary.

Thematically the album was a notable departure from the début, with Dolores now looking further afield for her lyrical inspiration. At the same time there was a degree of over-simplification that would normally have embarrassed even the most straightforward punk three-chord band by being piously banal and predictable, but she dealt with it in such a fashion that she got away with it. For example, the single 'Zombie' was about the Troubles in Northern Ireland, hardly a new lyrical topic, and one which many have fallen foul of (see The Police's 'Invisible Sun' and Simple Minds' dreadful 'Belfast Child'), but The Cranberries managed to deal with it reasonably well, despite at times using painfully obvious lyrical images. It was a song written in the immediate aftermath of the Warrington bombings by the IRA, which claimed the lives of several innocents including a young child. The track developed during soundchecks on tour and by the time it was recorded it had become a playful grunge restraint, with enough genuine passion to stop it lapsing into parody and cliché. In the press Dolores said it was a song that she felt was as applicable to Bosnia and Rwanda or any warring state as it was to Northern Ireland – all this smacked of a self-righteousness that has riddled some pompous acts, but The Cranberries dealt with it

tastefully and respectfully. Moreover, she did not shy away from potential critics who suggested she was walking on thin ice: "I think I am in a position where if you feel strongly about something and it really annoys you then other people will think the same as you and something can be done about it. But first you have to be aware before you do anything about it." Her respect for the issue was perhaps best demonstrated by the band's decision not to film their part in the video in Belfast, as they felt it was not appropriate to film the video promo for a pop single on streets which had been witness to so much death (instead they were filmed in LA and this was interwoven with footage of Belfast).

'Ode To My Family' was similarly a track that could have wallowed in sentiment but never did – it was written at a time on the road when their welcome success was threatening to keep them away from their beloved families for even longer. It spoke of lost childhoods, a troubled, sad but joyous track that made for an uncomfortable single. There was inner turmoil

on 'I Can't Be With You' and 'No Need To Argue' but there was also some slightly happier material with the ode to her husband 'Dreaming My Dreams', perhaps the album's only lighter moment. This track's wistful meanderings and orchestral touches were both hopeless and sweet, dealing with aspects of both love and loss. 'Icicle Melts' berated child murderers and '21' discussed how strange it is to grow old. 'False' was a beautifully understated acoustic piece, utterly radiant. The album's best moment was on the haunting 'Empty' a destitute sentiment delivered in rich, beautiful tones.

All of this was delivered in her gift of a voice, an instrument that made even her most banal lyrics poetic. The range was extended on this album, with Dolores swinging from sheer blissful singing to African wailing to virtual talking. Her performance was simply stunning, capricious, unique, abandoned and radiant, imbuing the most routine lyrics with total artistic worth and automatic profundity. Fortunately, the band were in top form as well, and without this she would have been at a loss – they formed a perfect foil for her extraordinary talent. The guitars were all suitably controlled, the string arrangements clipped and subtle and the overall tone very much one of a sophisticated simplicity. Stephen Street was again producing and his style helped by drawing out the key sections in the mix and ensuring that the occasional arpeggio overdose never became tinny or annoying.

With the band's international profile now so high, The Cranberries did not have to fear a repeat of the debacle that followed their début album's release. 'No Need To Argue' hit Top 10 in America, made No. 1 across most of Europe (where sales were mammoth), and was kept off No. 1 in the UK only by a resurgent R.E.M.. Within six weeks of its October 1994 release, it had sold 1.5 million copies. Within six months it had sold over 5 million, a phenomenal success. Double platinum status in the USA was followed by platinum in the UK and even gold in Canada. The Cranberries were now rivalling Madonna as one of the most MTV friendly acts – a superb MTV *Unplugged* appearance complemented a shelf-full of MTV Awards that followed this album (the MTV appearance will be released in 1995). They appeared to enormous applause at the massive Woodstock 2 festival and the tours for the album were sold out in record time.

The singles from the album were also massive successes: 'Zombie' was a Top 15 UK hit and earned the 'Most Played Radio Record' on the *Billboard* ratings in America. The second single 'Ode To My Family' in November was a similar smash as was the third release 'I Can't Be With You', which only confirmed their world-wide acclaim and their status as one of the biggest acts in the world. On a lighter note, the band were featured in a fashion spread in *Rolling Stone*, and Madonna announced that she was a big fan. Also, Dolores appeared on Jah Wobble's single 'Becoming More Like God', and managed to steal the limelight from the artist with her superb backing vocals. At concerts fans were widely seen to be crying at her words, and the merchandise sold so well they even offered a Cranberries condom for sale among the more traditional t-shirts and tour programmes.

The band's huge success and Dolores' growing star persona, fuelled the rumours that a split was impending and inevitable. These whispers had dogged the group since their inception, but they were much more widespread now. There was, in fact, good reason to believe that she was heading for a solo career. After all, here was a platinum blonde who challenged all the preconceptions about that image while singing songs of such emotion in a voice from the gods. Live, with her crystal voice and numerous costume changes, she was the focus. On record, her voice was the nucleus of the appeal and in interviews everyone wanted to talk to her.

The three men's stand-offish manners and reticence in interviews was well-known. Furthermore, they remained apparently unaffected by their success, whereas she had changed dramatically. The three men still lived with their parents – indeed, when the royalties finally came through from the success of the début album, the Hogan brothers moved their family lock, stock and barrel into a new and bigger house for all of them. On stage the brothers remained very much in the background, and their sullen looks and static style made them an unlikely accompaniment to the superwaif up front. Moreover, Dolores had now established herself as the main songwriter, whereas on the début she had shared more of the burden with Mike. The three musicians even joked in the press that their next album would be credited to "Dolores O'Riordan and the three other fellas".

Along with this apparent misfit, there was Dolores' changing image and lifestyle. Some said she was becoming arrogant – she had always been individual and strong-willed, but now there was more talk of her star petulance, with tales of tyrannical tantrums in rehearsals and soundchecks. In the live video released in late 1994, it is Dolores who hogs the screen and holds the centre of attention. Her multi-ear-ringed look and celebrity marriage fascinated the press, while the other three could walk down any high street in Britain and America without being noticed. While they appear to have become more subdued, with their Irish Catholic roots refusing to be swayed by the rock 'n' roll way of life, she has become more glamorous with each success, rapidly acquiring all the traditional star trappings such as a personal wardrobe assistant and a doting husband. She has even taken to referring to herself in the third person, such as saying "I always put Dolores first" in that absurd star fashion.

Press comments have accentuated the belief that she is harbouring a bloated sense of her own importance – when the band won a UK platinum record for the second album, she was quoted as saying "We didn't lose our heads over it because platinum's only 300,000 over here, it's one million in the States." Statements such as these hardly dampen rumours of her growing conceit. And other people in the industry talked of her tight money control, and of how she had sung backing vocals for Moose on one song and had allegedly harangued her manager for fees for months afterwards. Also, the press were angry at her apparent hypocrisy towards them. On the one hand she complained about press intrusion in her private life throughout 1994, such as after the pre-Christmas whirlwind tour of the USA, when the band had to cancel a small tour of Ireland because her badly damaged leg was suffering. The Irish press attacked her for this and stationed a zoom lens photographer outside her house. On the other hand, she appeared to revel in the attention – her own marriage could not have been more high profile and tailor made for the paparazzi.

Despite all this, Dolores denies she will turn solo, and apparently remains firmly committed to the band, without whom it has to be said, she would not have been where she is. In her own words, she feels solo careers are a pure self-indulgence: "I wouldn't like to be a soloist. It's bad for people to be on their own because they get very selfish." To be fair, she has had to appear in front of thousands of people world-wide, and without a strong degree of self-belief and confidence she would have been destroyed – the shy girl who started the band and was petrified by 20 people in a dark gig could simply not have handled 25,000 screaming fans in stadiums across the world. Maybe her change is forced, one borne of survival. Whichever way, the imminent solo career remains mere gossip.

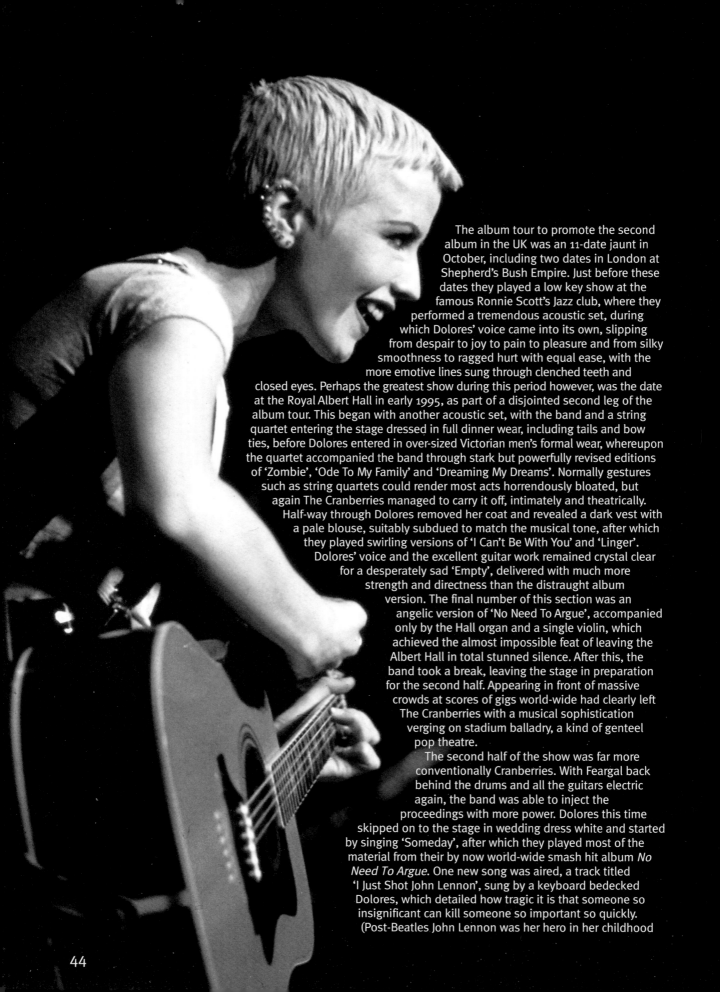

The album tour to promote the second album in the UK was an 11-date jaunt in October, including two dates in London at Shepherd's Bush Empire. Just before these dates they played a low key show at the famous Ronnie Scott's Jazz club, where they performed a tremendous acoustic set, during which Dolores' voice came into its own, slipping from despair to joy to pain to pleasure and from silky smoothness to ragged hurt with equal ease, with the more emotive lines sung through clenched teeth and closed eyes. Perhaps the greatest show during this period however, was the date at the Royal Albert Hall in early 1995, as part of a disjointed second leg of the album tour. This began with another acoustic set, with the band and a string quartet entering the stage dressed in full dinner wear, including tails and bow ties, before Dolores entered in over-sized Victorian men's formal wear, whereupon the quartet accompanied the band through stark but powerfully revised editions of 'Zombie', 'Ode To My Family' and 'Dreaming My Dreams'. Normally gestures such as string quartets could render most acts horrendously bloated, but again The Cranberries managed to carry it off, intimately and theatrically. Half-way through Dolores removed her coat and revealed a dark vest with a pale blouse, suitably subdued to match the musical tone, after which they played swirling versions of 'I Can't Be With You' and 'Linger'. Dolores' voice and the excellent guitar work remained crystal clear for a desperately sad 'Empty', delivered with much more strength and directness than the distraught album version. The final number of this section was an angelic version of 'No Need To Argue', accompanied only by the Hall organ and a single violin, which achieved the almost impossible feat of leaving the Albert Hall in total stunned silence. After this, the band took a break, leaving the stage in preparation for the second half. Appearing in front of massive crowds at scores of gigs world-wide had clearly left The Cranberries with a musical sophistication verging on stadium balladry, a kind of genteel pop theatre.

The second half of the show was far more conventionally Cranberries. With Feargal back behind the drums and all the guitars electric again, the band was able to inject the proceedings with more power. Dolores this time skipped on to the stage in wedding dress white and started by singing 'Someday', after which they played most of the material from their by now world-wide smash hit album *No Need To Argue*. One new song was aired, a track titled 'I Just Shot John Lennon', sung by a keyboard bedecked Dolores, which detailed how tragic it is that someone so insignificant can kill someone so important so quickly. (Post-Beatles John Lennon was her hero in her childhood

and still is.) At various stages she asked the audience to sing along, but this was hardly anthemic rock, and the crowd soon reverted to cigarette lighters and swaying with their arms aloft, while Dolores conducted them from above. For 'Daffodil Lament' there was a floral backdrop, then they rocked out again for a storming reprise of 'Zombie' which featured Dolores dancing in her odd way – a combination of an Irish jig and a Highland fling – and which in this context dispelled any shreds of soppy liberalism to become a heartfelt plea for peace. A giggle ridden version of The Carpenters' 'Close To You' followed a love drenched 'Linger' and by now the audience was bewildered by the sheer strength and quality of the show. With a shout of "Thank you, I love you" the petite Dolores led the band offstage to a standing ovation, blowing kisses and making the peace sign as she went. This was all a long, long way from that terrible night at Camden Underworld when the young band fumbled their way through a terrified set and thereafter saw all their dreams disintegrate before their very eyes. If any show to promote their second album encapsulated exactly what they were about, where they had come from and where they might be heading, this triumphant Royal Albert Hall concert was it. It was a truly breathtaking performance.

With a frightening tour itinerary for 1995, The Cranberries look set to spread their gospel still further in the future. Their journey from obscurity to becoming the biggest Irish musical export since U2 has been a bizarre and strange rush through managerial wrangles, stereotyped and disastrous press campaigns, personal illnesses and record flops, to multi-platinum sales, world-wide acclaim and huge celebrity. Perhaps more than any other band of recent times,

The Cranberries have had to persevere in America while Britain laughed and chided, until their heavy touring and classic yet modern sound finally paid off.

The belated success of *Everybody Else...* set them on a road to fame and stardom that rivalled any of the bands that had initially overtaken them in the UK, and proved that their sights were always set much higher than the patronising interviews and preconceptions of the early days. Ironically, after being guarded as a press secret, they are now one of the most popular bands on the planet. The combination of constant MTV exposure and non-stop touring provided a catalyst for their overwhelming success in the States. For a band once so derided as bumpkins, they are now well-travelled internationalists. Dolores has metamorphosed from a pathologically shy girl into a fledgling superstar, and has been compared to every great female lyricist along the way. But she has now established herself as one of the most distinctive female voices in rock history.

The Cranberries never have been, and never will be, cool or sexy. They have no hidden agenda, they don't even give good press. Despite all this, they have superseded the many fashionable acts around them with their music. The delicacy of their work and the stunning lush lilting voice that delivers the lyrics of heartache and romance mean they render all conceptions of fickle chic absolutely obsolete. By managing to be esoteric without being *avant garde*, they have captured the mainstream while never completely being immersed within it, straddling the traditional and the new with colossal success, heaping triumph on triumph. In five years they have been whisked from obscurity, publicly adored, sent bruised and battered back to obscurity, then ripped from that again into the harsh light of international stardom.

Along this whole strange journey The Cranberries have managed to negotiate their way through with their precious integrity intact, and within the absurdity and backlash that is today's pop world, that is a rare feat indeed.

DISCOGRAPHY

Singles

**Uncertain/Nothing Left At All
/Pathetic Senses/ Them**
Xerica XER14T (EP)
1991

Dreams/What You Were
Island IS548
(reissued on IS594 April 1994) (7")
November 1992

Dreams/What You Were/Liar
Island 12IS 548 (also on CD CID
548 reissued on CID 594 April 1994) (12")
November 1992

Linger (single version)/Reason
Island IS556 (7")
February 1993

**Linger (single version)/Hon
(Radical Mix)**
Island 12IS 556
(also on CD CID CID 556) (12")
February 1993

Linger (album version)
Island LINGCD1 (promo only)
December 1993

Linger/Pretty
Island IS559 (7")
January 1994

**Linger (live)/I Still Do (live)/
Waltzing (live)/ Pretty (live)**
Island 10IS559 (also on CD CID559) (10")
January 1994

**Not Sorry (live)/Wanted (live)/
Dreams (live)/Liar (live)**
Island CIDX 594 (CD)
May 1994

Zombie/Away
Island IS600 (7")
September 1994

Zombie/Away/I Don't Need
Island CID600 (CD)
September 1994

**Zombie (Full-length album version)/
Waltzing Back (live)/Linger (live)**
Island CIDX 600 (CID 600 and CIDX 600 also
came in a box labelled The Zombie Set, also
numbered CIDX 600) (CD)
September 1994

Ode To My Family/So Cold In Ireland
Island IS601 (7")
November 1994

**Ode To My Family/So Cold In Ireland/
No Need to Argue/ Dreaming My Dreams**
Island CID601 (CD)
November 1994

Ode To My Family (live)/Dreams
(live)/Ridiculous Thoughts (live)/
Zombie (live)
Island CIDK601 (CD)
November 1994

**I Can't Be With You/(They Long To Be)
Close To You**
Island IS605 (7")
February 1995

**I Can't Be With You/(They Long To Be)
Close To You/Empty** (BBC session)
Island CID 605 (CD)
February 1995

**I Can't Be With You (BBC session)/Zombie
(Acoustic)/Daffodil Lament (live)**
Island CIDX 605 (CD)
February 1995

Albums

**EVERYONE ELSE IS DOING IT, SO
WHY CAN'T WE?**
I Still Do/Dreams/Sunday/Pretty//Waltzing
Back/Not Sorry/Linger/Wanted/Still Can't.../I
Will Always/How/ Put Me Down
Island ILPS 8803 (LP) CID 8003 (CD)
March 1993

**VOLUME 9 (Various artist compilation,
plus book)**
How (live)
VOL 9VCD9 (CD)
March 1994

**NO NEED TO ARGUE
(Sampler, promo only mini-album)**
Zombie/Empty/Dreaming My Dreams/Daffodil
Lament/No Need To Argue
Island CRANCD1 (CD)
September 1994

**IF I WERE A CARPENTER
(various artists compilation)**
Close to You
A&M CD540258-2 (CD)
September 1994

NO NEED TO ARGUE
Ode To My Family/I Can't Be With You/ Twenty
One/Zombie/Empty/Everything I Said/The
Icicle Melts/Disappointment/Ridiculous
Thoughts/Dreaming My Dreams/Yeats' Grave/
Daffodil Lament/No Need To Argue
Island ILPS 9029 (LP) CID 8029 (CD)
October 1994

**WOODSTOCK '94 (Various artists
compilation)**
Dreams (live at Woodstock)
A&M 54032-2 (CD)
November 1994

PRET-A-PORTER (Various artists)
Pretty (remix)
Columbia COL 478226-2 (CD)
February 1995

**BBC1 RADIO SESSION: VOL 2
(Free tape with *Vox* Magazine)**
Zombie (radio version)
Vox CD GIVEIT 10
February 1995